BROKEN COLOR

Also by Dean Kostos

POETRY

Pierced by Night-Colored Threads

This Is Not a Skyscraper (recipient of the Benjamin Saltman Award, selected by Mark Doty)

Rivering (finalist, Gival Award)

Last Supper of the Senses

The Sentence That Ends with a Comma

Celestial Rust

PLAY

Box-Triptych

CHORAL TEXT

Dialogue: Angel of Peace, Angel of War

ANTHOLOGIES

Pomegranate Seeds: An Anthology of Greek-American Poetry

Mama's Boy: Gay Men Write about Their Mothers

SHORT FILM

Subway Silk

MEMOIR

The Boy Who Listened to Paintings

BROKEN COLOR

Dean Kostos

MADHAT PRESS
CHESHIRE, MASSACHUSETTS

MadHat Press
MadHat Incorporated
PO Box 422, Cheshire, MA 01225

The Library of Congress has assigned
this edition a Control Number of
9781952335174

ISBN 978-1-952335-17-4 (paperback)

Text by Dean Kostos
Author photo by Sofia S. Kostos
Cover design by Marc Vincenz
Cover image: *The Fifth Element,* mosaic by Gary Drostle,
www.drostle.com

www.madhat-press.com

First Printing

For Molly Peacock

Table of Contents

Life is not light but refracted color

—Johann Wolfgang von Goethe

CHAPTER ONE
SAP GREEN

The Doll God

In my Genesis reversed, I created females
first, then families of toilet-paper dolls.

I twisted heads, torsos, limbs,   smudged
pastel faces. Scrawled names on backs.

I hid the dolls in a box beneath my bed.
They aged, grew ill,

died. Some committed suicide,
some killed.

Dressed in the green of a Greek priest, I chanted
with a censer *Doll-ios, Death-ios*

& buried the dolls in sand
below our backyard swings. I stabbed

twig markers. Returning
in a red robe, I dug up

the remains—needing to see
death:

chewed, putrefied flesh. I reburied
the homunculi in the creek's clay banks

beside our house. Swamp-willow braids
swayed,   swept the ground.

Nights, I peered from my room. Muskrats
the size of chihuahuas patrolled the tombs.

Like tutelary spirits, the animals
swarmed. But I knew my dead dolls

were sealed from harm: clay
hardening by day & darkness.

Us-ward

I wade in boyhood's creek.
Currents reverse.   My parents grow
younger. Dusk. Crickets rasp. With one foot

in childhood, one in adulthood, I enter
night's tarnish & peer
into shuttered windows.

My parents rise from the cracked smile
they tried to inhabit. Their voices roar
us-ward.

I trace a path to the chatoyant creek.
Discolored currents.
Clay banks curve below a bridge

reeking of tar.
I scribble synonyms
for forgetting:

letter never signed,   letter
never sent to childhood's house.
That building is now a scar.

Cartographer of Laceration

No one knew I noosed my neck, one foot off a chair—
the other pointed

toward infinity. "Eleanor Rigby"
throbbed from my radio, halted

my leap. Cellos knifed my brain,
loosened death's necktie.

I became the pit into which I sank.
If someone only knew

my boy self—scarified
with boundaries, etched by neighbors

who shooed me from their lawns. I never protested,
respecting the tall words of adults.

If someone only knew how I became the cartographer
of laceration: razor, knife, shard.

Because blood's rose spiraled down
the sink, I bandaged my arm.

If I only knew how
self-loathing disfigures. The boy I was

still hides in memory like a gun smuggled
in the stomach of a dead cow.

The Man Who Wore His House as a Belt

He imagined relics in the attic:
photos with serrated edges, a mute

flute, vinyl disks hissing, *No.*
A crow swooped in black embrace

less silkily than recalled.
The man claimed

his childhood house betrayed him,
called him a liar.

He needed to find what he never knew,
imagined a family who celebrated

together. Photographs
would prove that.

Voices
sang from a diamond needle,

hovered like a moon slashed by clouds.

The man
who wore the clapboard house

as a belt, lived
between two worlds.

His upper self taught him
Hopkins, Vermeer, Poussin—

his lower self, resistance:
a kick when trapped. Legs dangled

like roots, body halved
by the inability to escape & the need to do so.

Broken Cage

Winged with invisible plumes,
I float above myself to see
belief's contraptions.
Hinged, my ribcage is
a bird cage. Tongue plucked,
song silenced, bars bent. I hear
wind's howling requiem,
taste words' descant,
feel them on my lips.
Lightning-colored silk
buffets sky.
Flicker of a wing.
Rusty cage, mute
song: Philomela lives.

Daughter of Wind

I plucked a star anemone—
daughter of wind.

It filled the sky's dome,
imprinted with tarnished leaves.

Rains sluiced shallow freshets,
rinsed roots.

I inhaled the anemone to breathe
its wrinkled air.

Leaves lobed,
leaves speared. Polyphonous

winds chanted through childhood.
As a boy, I

eyed a fenced-in horse—
mane pale as moonlight.

Luminary blooms flung into dusk
like runes.

I Miss Mrs. Williams

for Emily Anne Williams

The papier-mâché dinosaur, knowing nothing
of Lascaux, clomped up the stairs
of the Philadelphia Museum of Art,
enjoying an imperial, Japanese tea ceremony,
&, finally, sprouting wings
to better appreciate Calder.

How I miss Mrs. Williams.
I remember she said she loved
old wooden palettes—how the aging
wood, caressed with linseed oil, would
become my friend. I still see
wooden easels constructed

against crisp autumn skies,
with a background of reddened trees
quavering in wind. These moments
will always be intact, held
in the four pine bars of a canvas.
I miss Mrs. Williams & wish

I could find refuge in her kitchen,
still redolent with Toll House cookies & clay.
With pearl eyes & newspaper skin,
I'd once again sprout wings & soar
above my cluttered adult life—landing,
perhaps, in a Corot, a Vermeer, a Rousseau.

11

Dean Kostos

The Coat That Wore a Man

after Top Coat, *a photograph by Sofia Kostos*

A long, black coat contained a man,
wool shielding from blizzards.
The man trudged through fog until he
disappeared. The coat remains, hung
from an empty closet, above

a ruined wall, the adjacent building
razed. The coat waits, as if
the vanished man will return,
slogging through rain & snow.
But no, the man will not come back, the coat

angled toward the future. Because coats know
nothing of time, the tweed holds the man's shape,
perspiration, flakes of snow, & the dog-scent
of rain embedded in wool. The garment's arms
flap in wind, as if it longed to rise again.

Like Demosthenes

Demosthenes had "an inarticulate and stammering pronunciation"
that he overcame by speaking with pebbles in his mouth and by
reciting verses to the ocean.

My parents rented a house near the sea.
Open windows inhaled the power
of sun & wind. At night, I stuttered a plea
to herds of waves—desperate boy on our
beach. Like the ancient orator, I'd shout
Heal my stutter, my words trapped by day.
I felt the ocean's purred response. Devout,
I knew it had agreed to help. Its display
of growl was my protection, not attack.
I returned each night but hid
this secret. Like waves, I slid back
to the sand's edge, delighted
by water's sway. I surrendered to radiant might.
Moon-healed, my words floated: *Ignite.*

CHAPTER TWO
Phthalo Blue

At Janus's Gate

after John Donne's "Batter My Heart"

I scribble this letter to the unknown, the *you*
at the end of my sentence, you who mend
dualities—sharp shards that bend
into faces' wing-shaped beards, new,
always occupying the instant, due
to clocks whose hands never end:
end their taunt & torment, for I'm unable to defend
my quests & questions, focused under glass: true,
& yet, from another tilt, they're all too fain
to grant me that which undoes me (enemy?),
but that too is the two of Janus, whom I call again,
thinking the result will vary—his gate screeching as I
enter & leave, unsure which is which, free
of chiaroscuro daubing my shade, my *me*.

Broken Color

after a photograph by the author, manipulated for dramatic effect

*

Impressionists stabbed paint in short
strokes, refracted violent

luminosity to spill over forms,
figures, flesh.

* *

Rising from the bank of a creek, a tree's
roots resemble Chinese characters.

Rhizomes tangle below a body
of water. Bark like elephant hide;

ripples,
puckered skin.

* * *

In this landscape that doesn't exist,
leaves explode—shrapnel

white, gray, indigo. A tree trunk slants
across the scene,

across time's border: Ashen colors evoke
the firebombing of Dresden.

* * * *

Branches anoint
a thicket of shattered wings.

Wind & sun blast
ferocious light, sear

an imprint: Face
on the Shroud of Turin.

Skies

I. Jacopo Tintoretto

Mosaic glinted gold
      till the Renaissance
      frescoed
blue.

Painters' depictions of sky
      mark their art.
      The Baroque whorls:
angels slice air

in horizontal flight.
      Cloud-nimbused,
      a man watches
wings scissor

indigo. Sails swell.
      When squalls thrash
      a boat, that man defeats
the storm,

walks the sea's
      diminuendo.
      In the distance,
robed figures glide

marble stairs.
As a woman's hand
guides a child,
a waterfall of stars weeps.

II. EL GRECO

Sun stabs muscular clouds.
Sky is shattered skin.
Skeletal buildings languish
   on the hillside of Toledo.

Trees twist under cumulonimbus.
Mannerist bodies writhe:
The *Laocoön*, a python
   coiling. Legs dissolve

into gray flames.
Sky sags under the weight
of spirit.
   In the Transfiguration,

flesh
is vapor,
is wind, is
   fire.

III. J. M. W. Turner

Clouds like the underbelly of a cat.
  Dawn blanches blue.
    Ocher scumbles air.
Sun blooms: chrysanthemum.

A mountain range carves seeing
  & sea. Teal darkens
    teal. A galleon's reflection,
autumned. The ship tilts toward

the depths of dry-brush
  & cyan smear.
    Wind uprights the vessel, sky
replaced by Venice.

23

IV. MARY CASSATT

There are always pairs: sky & air,
lakes & elms, parents & children.
Like a dragonfly, a turquoise bow
    attaches itself to a girl's braid.

Stippled oil & pastel—
sky's patina swarms. Sun gleams
into leaves, the pale
    blue vein of a temple.

Cobalt reflects on the fleshy
gloss of sand. Two
children, two parents,
    two steps forward, two back.

V. Edward Hopper

The sky always belongs to someone else—
    someone outside your window.
    Matte sapphire meets the eye
like a riddle. The impasto

becomes a wheat field.
    No end.
    A woman waits in a room
without people. A door swings

open to sea & sky. A monument
    of light questions the hour.
    Another woman: light-bathed,
stares into stratus. A palette knife

scrapes oil paint.
    Because no one inhabits the lighthouse,
    no one winds the clock. Voices
evaporate.

Dean Kostos

VI. Leonora Carrington

Like pepper & salt, two women,
   dressed in white & black, attend
   the wedding of shadow & vapor.
Sparrowy distances haunt

a sky. Cluster
   of towers. One woman has lost
   her face. Balance pervades this wedding
of statues with vacant eyes.

Charcoal clouds hunker
   over a house in silhouette. Emptiness
   fills emptiness. Cirrus suspended
above a white horse.

VII. FRIDA KAHLO

Blind as a blue petal, a face paints
itself into sky, unselving
the foment of color.
Ragged aura divides

two selves, performs
surgery, knits nerves. The painter
becomes a doe. Pierced with arrows
like Saint Sebastian, she shields

herself in a colonnade of trees.
Celadon sky squeaks through,
peers like an eye:
Day of the Dead.

When her bifurcated body is sutured
with white leather straps,
her spine becomes a Doric column,
her voice a celebration.

VIII. Paula Rego

Is Lisbon's cardboard sky
      pinned into place
      by the moon?
Arm-in-arm, dancers lean

like mannequins, skewered with metal rods.
      Soldiers pry themselves
      from storybooks.
Costumes shed like stalks.

The dancers gather, beam
      through windows. A gray
      flame brackets a woman.
She breathes its ether.

IX. Francis Bacon

The absence of sky falls
into a screaming mouth.
Like scorched wings, a halved
        carcass looms behind a man.

        Faces collapse & eat themselves.
The stygian, taupe, gray
of Manet. Swooping curves
        carve a face.

        Pulp. Murmur.
An orange room, darkened
with caskets, closes in.
        Shade. Smear.

        Watching from an oblique angle,
a mason studies
the blueprint of a house
        without windows, without sky.

CHAPTER THREE
PAYNE'S GRAY

The Finisher Speaks to Charon

A finisher handsews linings, pockets, & clasps onto fur coats.

No longer alive, my hand
is a flame. Embroidered wings arc
beyond all, floating.… Who

I was & am remains an unvoiced question.
Haloed in apricot light, I see
the former work of my body: suturing

satin into fur coats. Needle
in hand, I stitched at home
to send money to family in Greece.

But you knew me long before:
a braided girl, supporting my family with my loom.
Married, my husband trundled me to America.

You knew me when my he
forced me to drag weights to abort my babies.
You tucked each fetus into your robe.

I moaned guilt's litany & wept
into a black-bordered handkerchief
when my husband's heart erupted, cradled

in my daughter's arms. Their *Pietà*.
Years passed. She married in a blizzard of veils.
A dark column, I planted seeds

33

of light. My last day, I maundered
your name, *Charon, take me.* I couldn't peel
my eyes from you, invisible

to all but me. When death rattled, you
gathered me in your arms.
I smelled your incense breath

when I slipped from form.
Into an ocean of arpeggios,
I nestled into the leaf of soul.

How membrane-thin
the wall between flesh & lumina.
Those in form don't know

how close we are.
We swim the dialogue between realms.
I embroider gnosis, thread

& fiber. From the brocade
whorling on your sleeve,
you, Charon, offer me your hand.

Charon's Response

for Anna Kontogeorgiou

My voice uncoiled like smoke,
hand unspooling bolts.
I changed with the whorl
of damask.
My name faded:

"Hare mou, pare me," you sewed with breath.

Myrrh scent. Shirred shadow.
Wings' brush. You were a girl
at a loom, feet not reaching
the floor. Olive leaves culled soot. Mines
ate your father's lungs.

"Hare mou, pare me," you wove wet eyelashes.

When your husband died,
you pressed tears
between pages. Grief's
rage burned holes
into black handkerchiefs.

"Hare mou, pare me," you embroidered the Virgin's hair.

At your apartment altar,
your arms fragrant with anise,
you told your daughter's
son village tales:
the girl with pomegranate cheeks,

an almond tree
chanting the moon's
hagiographa. The boy
called you *Yiaya,* Grandmother.
An arthritic olive tree writhed

toward eternity. Roses mouthed Jesus's
wounds. You taught
the boy to pray—wedded
spirit with breath, as you
did the last day:

"Hare mou, pare me," you chanted.

A white *sávano*
gown floated round you. Slipped
from sleep, you nested,
your head crowned,
luminous.

"Hare mou, pare me ..."

Despite devotion to the Virgin Mary,
you pinned your eyes to my pagan face.
I gathered you in my arms, a bride
across the threshold,
surrendered.

Gnosis

The psyche knows itself in the corridors
    of green mirrors,

steps into cool waters.
    Meets itself

in half-lit hallways:
    imprints pollen paths.

The self
    dips to drink,

its face melting, reformed.
    Mind's

jagged extremities.
    The soul knows itself

by itself,
    feet plashing.

Archaic Smile

Folklore
has a word for
"shadows," the kind I tug
from my mouth when half asleep. I've
been to Greece

in the past, seen
its ancient sites
but did not know
the *Kritios Boy*. His tilt
freed

him to
step from marble.
I swam to the statue's
archaic smile—half grin, grimace.
I curved

into
his paradox.
A jewel-eyed peacock shrieked
like the screech of a gate.
When the

moon stained
words on strangers'
doors, voices wailed
inscrutable names.
Unheard.

Yannis Ritsos

Mouthing a skein of cigarette smoke,
you faced the Acropolis. It bled

a swastika. You scoured the blood
of ghosts,

wrote with blue that veins paper,
with rust that reddens soot.

When compass roses grew thorns,
maps darkened.

After Nazis emptied banks
& pilfered food, you boiled soup from stones.

Mouths mute as Philomela's
jawed. Curfews inflicted.

Because Archbishop Damaskinos forged
baptismal records: Athenian Jews fled.

Four years in a prison camp, you wrote elegies
with cursive fumes.

Goats' tongues shriveled
from thirst. Groves of olive trees burned.

When you tore a page,
poems hemorrhaged. Mouths

dimmed with rage. Sleeves
of knitted script unraveled.

Fists seized the syntax of smoke.
After 22 Nobel refusals, your papers

drank ink. On the grounds
that you were a Communist, lies

poured into veins. Civil war ensued,
children's eyes bandaged.

The Junta wiped blood from chalices.
Cracked lips swilled prayer.

When a pen knifed your brain
to the ground, you stained paper

with the imprint of your psyche.
Eyes winced.

As the Aegean exhaled,
you spat spirit from blood.

Dean Kostos

At the National Gardens, Athens

I live through my eyes.
Apricot-colored light

secretes from columned Zappeion Hall.
I crane my neck to see

the statue of Lord Byron, "gloomy egoist."
He shakes off his marble skin & climbs from the plinth.

I thank him for his sacrifice to Greece's
independence, recite octaves from *Don Juan*.

His marble sheen reflects present & past.
We rove corridors of knobby vines.

In response to the poet's presence,
butterflies flicker in clouds of bougainvillea.

Dark doves murmur from pines, scent
of late-summer musk, of semen.

Oranges pattern the ground, rot among petals.
The doves fall silent

as dusk seeps through crosshatched branches.
The poet returns to his plinth.

Church bells echo my thoughts: *alone,*
all one.

Monarch butterflies close their wings
like eyelids.

In the Town of Delphi

Not far
from Pythia's
tripod, she inhaled
methane fumes & fell into a trance.
Mount Parnassus

stabs the sky.
I climb hillside stairs, see
a terracotta sea of roofs.
Cypress spires carve clouds. I
watch a hearse

snake down the street.
White-flowered wreathes.
Ribbons inscribed
with names. In the chapel, women
grasp photos,

ex-votos.
The funeral might as
well be a wedding. No longer
pagan, frescoed icons
 scratch nails into plaster

as they climb the dome.
Theotokos
emerges, fills
the golden concave.
I pad to an arched veranda.

My eyes' thirsty sparrows
drink dawn's phantom.
The Pythia's vision has freed us.
Plato's cave, after all,
was his skull.

Motion Observed:
Eadweard Muybridge

I.

Balancing a basket of emptiness, a woman
emerges from shadow,

multiplies. Nudes sacrifice
themselves to time.

Carrying an alabaster bowl
filled with water & laurel,

a man becomes many men. A woman
appears in rows of stop-motion

photographs, cradles stalks of lilac,
chants anapests.

Each movement
is a photographic freeze-frame,

a sliver of silver intelligence.
Bodies adhere to the act of action,

observed. Looking changes what is seen.
A fractured narrative speaks:

flesh & fullness. A man heaves
a medicine ball. A woman empties

a bucket of flickering light.

II.

Stooping, another woman throws
a wrap of diaphanous cloth

around her shoulders. It whorls
into faces—cherubim.

The woman dances, cloth arcing
into pinions.

As she spins,
the fabric flickers from white

to the iridescence on a pigeon's neck.
Light eludes

sight, fills fibers with kinesis.
With each stop-frame, her movements

shimmer into Linear A, still
undeciphered.

In her final stance, she petrifies
into the *Venus de Milo*.

Her arms grow back.

III.
Twelve stop-motion photographs.
The body determined

as an opera. An aria
spirals from a shellac disc. What is sung

is seen. "Descent" &
"ascent" reverse

as in Duchamp's *Nude Descending a Staircase:*
an accordion of steps collapses

in on itself. I enter the painting: breathe
burnt-umber air. Leaving, I hear

bodies speak the language of arrival.
Flesh becomes intellect.

Study of movement. Joints
bend into grammar.

What language does the body speak?
A model climbs a ladder, returns

with a rock in his hands,
carries the heft like a libation bearer.

Wires tripped by feet
discharge a phalanx of cameras. Studied,

locomotion magics mind.

CHAPTER FOUR
Alizarin Crimson

Agon, Ago

A pantoum inspired by *Beowulf, Sir Gawain & the Green Knight, Piers Plowman,* & the *York Play at the Crucifixion*

Unbeings' bones clatter into spears.
Yesternight, a cavalier
flailed but failed to shield.
The king dismounted his throne.

Yesternight came: A fallen knight,
lame, immured by castle walls.
The king vacates his throne.
Paladins shot arrows with the sun's ferocity.

Lame, the regent hid amid ramparts.
Ghosts glided.
Cavaliers cast spears.
The bishop missed, no jewel kissed.

Ghosts glided,
pierced by sabers.
The bishop slogged
into purgatory,

pierced.
Having flailed but failed to protect,
paladins trudged into purgatory.
Unbeings' shattered into spears.

Undoer Of Knots

Enveloped in clouds
of drapery, the Virgin
perches between injured

angels—pinions curved
like parentheses. Cherubim
polish scapular

feathers. A crescent
cradles her sandaled feet.
The tabernacled

multiverse: her realm,
her reign. Seraphs surround
her shoulders. With each thought,

a winged face alights.
Though the Virgin stands still, she's
in constant motion.

Her robe sways. Legions
of tutelary saints comb
plumes. Seraphic fists

bloom with anguish. Strand
by strand, they hand them to her.
She slips open pain's

ribbons, webs, nooses.
Her eyes tilt into hands' work:
bouquets of knots.

Oneiromancy

William Blake's engraving *Sullen Moloch* combined with a
dream

I.

Eyes see through knotted seams of sleep.
Verbs disappear.... Can't stop ~~staring;~~
muscles ~~erupt~~ from graphite.

Glowing red king. Scar man, scepter
in hand. Umbrella-wings above his head.
A worshipper ~~dances, wails.~~

~~Drowns~~ out screams. Tambourine in fist.
Adults slaughter toothless children. Dancers' robes ~~ignite;~~
white flames. A newborn ~~backs~~ into a flaming oven.

~~Sacrificed?~~

II.
Clunk! Metal doors bolt behind us.
Men in lab coats herd us
into a cinder-block bathroom.

Char dims rust-streaked walls.
Liquefied plaster oozes from corners,
a crust. I can't ~~see~~ the faces

of people in charge but hear them ~~bark~~
at us to ~~sit~~ on toilets. The seats
~~fuse~~ with our skin—a crackling

sound. Our flesh ~~takes~~ on the texture
of cuttlebone, dissolves
like a corpse in a sarcophagus.

No one ~~speaks,~~ mute mourning.
We ~~scab~~ into body shells, like victims
of Pompeii. Entombed in volcanic ash & pumice—

decayed away.
Our body shells ~~disappear,~~
~~sacrificed.~~

Gaze

words with the Latin root spectāre, *to look*

Making a spectacle of himself, an acrobat
leaps into gasps. Midsummer sun

somersaults with spectacular ferocity.
The body sings in summer.

Winter is introspective,
no longer the specter of puissance.

The gaze prospective, waiting
to reenter the sphere of solstice.

Looking into ice like an Italian mirror,
say *Specchio.*

Hope to see something perspicacious.
I've viewed the sun the way a spectator

gawps at a boxing match—curious, horrified.
Stepping back, I glimpse my spectral self,

shuttling like *Nude
Descending a Staircase.* It's the spectrum

of my life—childhood to old age. I climb
stairs toward light for perspective.

Etymologia

words from Greek roots

Take a metaphor to the top floor
        & park your car in the thesis. Listen

to the man with a wooden voice
        murmuring through a xylophone.

His words are an anthology of chrysanthemums,
        budding midair.

Is it a goat's song, a tragedy, or will it ascend
        a chromatic scale, a flight of stairs—

colors booming? Giving an aristocratic
        apostrophe, he turns down a path,

heading toward catastrophe. In the gloom,
        his skull beams like a theater, his eyes

viewing the glister of theory. Call
        it an epiphany, rising like the sun's aura

after rain. Some may even call
        it fantasy, but, like an amputated

arm flexing its fingers,
        it's a phantom, a phantasm.

Bruges

Beguiled by the name resembling *bruise,*
I fly to Belgium. A train whisks

me to a museum
where paintings whisper

through cracks. I dissolve into a triptych.
Women wear wimples, men

luxuriant silks.
Dead painters' hands tug at me,

persuade me to confront
my younger self.

Emerging from a portrait's impasto,
my doppelganger floats toward me.

Centuries crumble: I become his father.
He waits outside the museum. Needing

his forgiveness, I summon his gaze.
Canals glaze. Mansard roofs contain books

inked with brown blood.
As poplars bend in wind,

swords of forsythia slant.
A punt glides along the canal.

My double nods, *Enter.*
A lit basilica asserts spires against night.

Vertical silence reflects my double:
He does what I fear doing,

speaks what I fear saying.
His voice peals. Unseen,

he slips between threads of rain,
curves into me like a fetus.

Medicinal Corridors

The Mütter Museum, Philadelphia

Daguerreotype of a man,
        withered horn curving

from his forehead. Forearms—long as thighs,
        thin as wrists. Vitrines present parades

of dwarf skeletons. Bones glister,
        sinister jewelry.

As I leave,
        fragments grin.

A six-foot colon looms
        in a glass casket like a sunburned iguana.

Rows of skulls gaze from sockets'
        sepulchers.

The wax replica of another man leans
        back, reveals his throat: sliced smile, flayed

pink & white muscles, nerves
        complex as electrical circuitry

that didn't exist in his lifetime. Peering
        back two centuries,

I'm greeted by a face in a jar—severed
        from the head it adorned,

from the person who called it
        "I." The face has the shape & shade

of an Anjou pear, suspended in formaldehyde
        by pins' parentheses. Eyes

point downward in regret. Lips part,
        preparing to say, "I was."

Dean Kostos

Fragments: Monsters on a Beach

An imaginary poem from the sixteenth century

I.

Their bodies are a grammar—each [   ] a letter.
It would be better
to begin with the monster off-center: he's
the headless one. *Please,*
pleads his torso [   ]

from the rest of me. My parts must walk together.
His body blushes [ ]:
A subject without its verb, I would cease.
My skeleton is grammar.

To the right, a monster [
                    ]
Posing, as if [   ]
hands into a killer's gloves, he sees
himself reflected in waves' lather,
reveals his glamour.

II.

Two monsters engage in conversation.
One: *How odd the ocean,*
so cold in July. The other: *How* [ ] *the sky.*
In [ ], a two-headed boy tries
to catch our attention.

This Janus-faced Cupid shuns
labels. His heads gaze East & West to nations
as he tries to diagram why
bodies of water [   ].

His mother runs to help her son.
[

                    ] She has only one eye
but hates the moniker "Cyclops." [
                    ] her coiffure of brains curls:
Grammar [   ] *glamour.*

III.

She delights in the way sun falls
on her face, which she tilts so as not to appall
us. Her hand
points [   ]

to the monster on her right. [   ]
[   ] All
he wants to do is blot out the sun scrawling
through clouds, etch a testament in sand:
An infected body is an inflected grammar.

[   ] face mauled,
he reads names of ogres to enthrall
[   ]
Turning toward the headless monster on the strand,
he yanks "t" from "that," offers him a "hat," [   ]
"Grammar not my body!"

Phobia Vessel

A brain flicker ballooned out, filling
the Gare du Nord. A bike pump wedged

in my skull expanded the station's space.
Felt like I'd explode, stretched

to squeakiness, my head whirling
off, hailing shards.

I first felt this nameless phobia in Paris,
nineteen & alone. From that day on, I can't enter

large, enclosed spaces. If I try,
one hundred hooves drum

my blood. A herd of executioners jeer
secrets about me. Passengers stream

by in suits & dresses, trundling trunks to safe
destinations. How jealous I was

& am. What bent my brain into yawning
space? Did the flattened balloons of

depressions swell inside me, their faces
rising like gaseous gargoyles?

Wish I could've emptied them.
But phobia's bulbous face grew & grows,

invading my brain, blocking entry
to airports, stations, cathedrals, museums.

I walk close to moldings,
clutch them like a mountaineer his cord.

I skulk in hallways to peer
at paintings I've traveled thousands of miles

to see. Panicked upon entering spacious galleries,
I view the paintings in gift-shop postcards.

I am the painting of a man with a crack
in his forehead.

His damage opens to a gasping
expanse. To vanquish panic, I blink

my eyes. Like the click of a tape measure,
coiling itself, my seeing spools inside me.

My eyes orbit. I'm a planet flung
from its track.

Will the Earth melt open, soft
as a kneaded eraser? Will I be erased

to a soul-glow smudge?
My outline effaced—me & not-me blurs,

uncontained. I am a mushroom cloud, spying
on my charred landscape:

Globes of smoke dot the road
where rage & terror collide.

My mind retraces childhood's
ruins, searching for abandoned rooms.

The sky is not my mother,
not a womb. It grows metallic,

cracks like Humpty-Dumpty's skull.
I glue his shards

around my rawness.
Vertiginous selves hiss,

"Vaster. You have no axis!
Faster—you have no access."

Self to Self

Wounds mouth, "Mend."
Today bends
in a funhouse mirror, each new
step a trajectory to
distortion. Each day ends
the everywhen of yesterday. Rend
your vanished past. Former Self pursues
fears never made manifest—sends
gentling words. Friend
to yourself, offer entreaties.
Peer through selves again.
Past You, seize
the "I" you are, its fragments free
of aloneness—cleansing breeze:
we.

The Ear Speaks, the Mouth Listens

Daimons in ancient Greece were considered divine powers, fates,
guardian spirits, or angels.

Sirens, horns, cursing. Commotion
erupts from New York's relentless motion.
An outstretched hand. Hordes shun,

eyes avert. Shrieking manifold:
city I speak & hear, hidden in wounds' folds.
Daimons pierce schist, an old

belief in spirits rising from soil. I stumble
over superstition. Sun's arrows tumble
from clouds, stab the way a picador lances a bull.

One life defeats another—victor deemed important.
Chimerical sunsets spill red over skyscrapers: portent
of unhealed wounds. Sky becomes a tent

over daimons recalled, eliminated
by generations passing through thought's liminal
scrim. Sirens hymn: null.

Dean Kostos

Waking

A knife peels open
day's edge, pulp of radiance.
I curl from sleep's rind.

Its fragile crust turns
the color of a locust's
shell. Sky swallows sun's

fruit. I curl,
drowse: last nugget of sleep
dissolves on my tongue.

Voices Sieved

vibrate
a wave
of bees
buzz clouds
cool tears
bend tongues
in bells
loll screams
vast space
trapped in
stations
cracked street
tenors
sieved hum
speak the
threshold
of noose
hour of
cellos
phones weep
laments
unheard

Dean Kostos

David Byrne

From a series of digital portraits by Lucas Samaras, Poses. *The Pace Gallery, New York, 2010*

Your face:
invitation
to gray fire, dissolving
was, will be. Photographed black &
white, your

head is
a George Hurrell
portrait of a rock, dredged
from the Hudson. Hidden beneath
waters,

silver
magma ignites.
Your eyes are libation
vessels sacrificed to night's dark
flames. Wind,

cinders.
The color
is collar—brown among
resolute ash. The zipper at
your neck

lets word-
sparks fly—neither

spoken nor sung—from the
cage confining, defining them,
you. Us?

CHAPTER 5
OCHER

A Woman Shaving Her Temples

after a woodblock print by Utamaro

The body is poised
calligraphy. Undulations
swoon into speech. Glance

from mother to child.
Erasing hair with a blade,
the woman dusts her neck.

Like a ginkgo root, the
Chinese character for *origin*
adorns her throat.

Grooming is a language—
hair-combs, elegiac. Drapery
falls in fugitive

tints of peach & bruise.
Formlessness inspirits form.
The boy sees himself

in his cursive mother.
Plump as a bud, he seeks her praise.
By a singed window,

by a smudged mirror,
the boy listens as stillness
refuses to respond.

Dean Kostos

Awabi Fishers

after a woodblock print by Utamaro

Wet hair bleeds
down her back, as if the blade
had slipped from her mouth

& slashed her. All is water:
ocean, glistening strands
of hair, the cloth

she wrings dry. Her teeth clasp
the blade to shuck shell-fish.
A crouching woman

offers a shell
with ragged edges,
gestures *Try one.*

The basket is full.
Sea scent weaves
through air &

waves. Sand swallows feet.
The woman arranges
shells to the brim.

Unlike the other
woman, this one's body is
concealed in florid

80

textile: iris, spider lily.
Her hair is a pagoda
of black gloss. She

knows she must act now—finally
touch her friend.
They've known each other

for years, but she's hidden
her affections.
The ocean breathes out & in,

as if to draw the women close.
This panel is one of three,
a triptych. Do the women

know that the section
where they've spent centuries
fishing is incomplete?

Does a *before* & an *after*
exist in the missing panels?
The desired touch may remain

forever out of the kneeling
woman's reach. Her
gown's muddied dye, bleeding.

The Hobby Horse

after a woodblock print by Harunobu

In this print, let's pretend
the woman is the mother. She steps
from a block of wood,
freed by the artist's gouge.
The umbrella in her hand tilts

over her son. A hobby horse
lurches beneath his legs
as if to result in arrival.
But distance means nothing
as cherry blossoms scour

the sky. Clouds of camellias rise
from a bamboo screen.
We are privy to glimpse
only a slice of the scene.
Orange & auburn repeat

throughout the print: stripes
on the horse's robe, a pleat
on the mother's kimono.
Instead of pleasure pearling
her face, her profile blurs.

Dusk dissolves as she imagines
she can fade away (bent
in obeisance).

But no.
The umbrella protects

from nothing,
The horse arches his neck.
As Earth slants,
the rocking boy knows
he is going nowhere.

Dean Kostos

Moso & the Bamboo Shoots

after a woodblock print by Koryusai

Chrysanthemums of snow
bloom above a bamboo
gate. A woman holds
an umbrella over herself,
a man shoveling. He

uncovers ripe
bamboo shoots for a soup
his grandmother brewed.
The umbrella resembles
a white hawk, wings spread.

As if the artist wants to show
how reality exceeds paper boundaries,
the falling snow
erases details. The man
chips at ice.

Could the gate
lead to a Shinto temple,
ashes chanted in a charred urn,
the cremated body housed
in clay?

The grandmother's
spirit spirals, hair in wind.
As voices thrum, fists scatter

salt onto snow to purify
what can't be seen.

Evening by the Sumida River

after a woodblock print by Kiyonaga

Currents babble behind
three women, kimonos
rippling. Gouged lines imply

gowns' sway.
Drapery cascades
in russet stripes.

Are these three women
or three aspects of *one:*
youth, middle age, senescence?

The young geisha
wears a black *obi*. Was she
pregnant? Did she choose

termination?
Is remorse ever forgotten?
Does the artist use this print

to make us look at
our anguished choices?
The women tilt

their faces, eyes turned toward unseen
shorelines. The river gurgles.
All three women wear

tortoise-shell combs.
Teeth devour waves of hair—
lustrous, lacquered, architectural.

The women
quicken steps.
The woodblock's grain suggests

clouds. In V-formation,
regrets migrate above the landscape.
Lights seep through shoji screens.

Geishas at the Niwaka Festival

after a woodblock print by Utamaro

Steam recedes like a scrim
rising from sulphur springs. Bathing
in cherry-&-clay soap, three women

prepare to attend a festival of mimes.
The geishas comb coiffures,
tuck them into translucent hats.

One woman gloves her hands.
Feathers sprout like blood jets.
Printed paper offers margins

beyond which ache fades.
Patterns flicker, colors
singed. Words evaporate

before the mimes step
on stage. Two women
look left: thoughts from their past.

A geisha snaps
open a fan. Drums pound.
A mime grasps air

to retrieve this instant,
knowing he never can.
Choreography of bones.

Returning Geese at Night

a woodblock print by Harunobu

As a shoji screen
rolls away, night descends
into black ink.

Geese in formation
point toward clouds. Leaves
ignite as green

flames bud on tree limbs.
Rain-bloated clouds. Stepping
on the veranda,

two sisters stand by a
balustrade, watching night's squall.
Beaks wail, *Again, ago.*

The younger girl
looks down—knows
years are marked by the coming

& going of leaves, storms, geese.
The older girl pivots
to return

to the bark-brown
house, her gown spilling
at her feet. She touches her

89

sister's shoulder. The
mournful squawk of geese
dissolves into thunder.

Pictures of the Floating World

for Ono No Komachi, after a woodblock print by Harunobu

Feeding paper's thirst
for living ink, she writes
instead of being
written about, fingertips
stained. Language

shuttles through her brain
as threaded fire weaves
through a loom. Her *obi*
—in colors of gourd—
conceals a manuscript.

Her poems awaken Noh ghosts
to writhe. This poet of the floating
world wears nobility's
green robe, a train
of white silk, stained

like a blemish.
From a horse-hair brush,
from an ink stone, a stork soars.
As the poet writes,
long hair inscribes her neck.

Despite early fame, her poems
dim, diminish.
The court revokes her brushstrokes

on mulberry paper.
Her lasting seal: chrysanthemum.

In poverty, in obscurity,
her vowels become wounds.
Wailing winds rage
through her skull's
eye sockets.

Soir Bleu: Six Perspectives

*a painting by Edward Hopper, Whitney Museum of American
Art, New York*

1. THE PROPRIETRESS

I govern this rectangle—boundaries push
into me, press moisture from my skin.
Behind the saturnine glow of my lipstick,
I wait. A galaxy of lamps

yaws above me. My eyes soar
through this smoky café,
alight on a businessman & courtesan,
tête-à-tête. She peers

from the balustrade, chocolate-
colored gown cascading.
He gobbles crème-caramel truffles,
fans a royal flush. He swigs

spiked espresso, snuffs Gauloises,
gestures to her. They rise. Vanish.
What is movement, orbit
from None to Numb?

Dean Kostos

2. The Courtesan

He & I ascend the *ascenseur.*
Hazed in smoke, our words float, lanterns.
Merlot floods my throat: voices
loud, waning, moaned....

I warm pearls but never ask:
how long married?
Other women? My dress puddles
onto parquet—my roan

chignon a dénouement.
With eyes closed, chocolate melts
on tongues.
Communion.

3. THE BUSINESSMAN

Charlotte ... Deirdre ...
Anne ... Chateau Pétrus.
More ganaches, more giandujas,
more pralines.

4. THE CLOWN

The owner thinks I don't see her—absurd.
I fan my regal hand, learned concealment.
I'm no magician, unless you count
years I've made disappear:

somersaulting, pitching tents, hammering
spikes into frozen soil.
Look: no smeared, ear-to-ear
greasepaint smile.

5. THE CARD SHARK

I roll a cigarette with spit
& contempt, eavesdrop on tips, chase
whiskey with burnt café noir.
I flourish false cuts, false shuffles.

6. My Eyes

My pupils are mouths:
I consume what I see.
Seeing is grammatical: the dependent
clause to the left, divided

by a pole—wing of a triptych by Robert Campin,
Flemish master. Forget
art history. *Soir Bleu* resists
symmetry, no second wing.

Isolated dramas erupt.
The Proprietress pricks
my gaze with coffee-black distance,
drowns.

Singing through Our Bones

Our mouths
sing through
ancient
marrow.
Words' chords
vanish
into
a flute.
Fixes
breath's song.
Sound waves
soon seek
escape.
The jet
of air
from mouths
travels.
Air waves
deflect
dried bones'
dried songs.

Glistening Scar

Line 100 rhymes with the first; line 99 with the second, etc.

I.

The meeting of *wont* and *won't* wars.
Thought's empire
enacts laws.
Corrupt ideas
fell
a country. A word's sword impales.
Ghostdom:
Hear them.
Flames bloom
fuchsia. Torture intrigues historians:
crucifix to mustard gas, deadly fragrance.
Cruelty's contraptions have multiplied since then.
Silhouettes
define what bodies forget.
Dirges sing praise.
Grayish
specters flee night's street.
Flight of Paraclete:
Heal hurt.
Behind a parapet,
panes
open, a demilune
suspended. Sorrow sings the *vox*
humana: Callas.
Voices shatter into static

II.
as torment anoints.
Confronts.
We find ourselves split
(dazed?),
seeking justice.
A smaze
clouds the mind. Cursive fonts
spell threat.
Vacant, the self is a shirt
fluttering past radiant
lamps. Lambent
spirits visit haunts.
As brain work leaks,
we disunite
& pray to varnished
versions of our past: absence.
Bronze statues announce
themselves with toothless
mouths ... moan.
Drowned
figureheads swoon.
Below water's skin,
coral resembles a brain.
Sanity's membrane
eludes us. We balance like an egret

III.

to forget
or attain
(in tercets & quatrains),
to learn who were are. In Manhattan,
hoards crowd noons.
In this jagged town,
cloned
faces
pronounce
life sentences.
The homeless perish.
Might
allows the accused to prevail. Bleak
lives mount
hearses. Lament....
Chants
rise like incense. In concert
halls, a lullaby transforms a requiem to let
mourning illuminate form. Gaunt,
Fauré
composed his anguish.
Music has a visual equivalent: a glaze
on portraits.
Brushstrokes create the stunt
of vision. The point:

IV.

imagistic music.
Museums open as
paintings unlock
moons.
Corot-light sprays like rain.
Sunsets
subvert
the self, the selfie. Heat
rises, repeats.
Wishes
dissolve into a haze.
A crosshatched etching is a net.
Let
us rinse
vengeance
till it ceases to rot. Viridian
leaves fall. Soon,
we defend nature over theorem,
beauty over brutality. A postmortem
reveals no thing. A trail
winds toward a place to dwell,
to yell, "Hosea,"
while lanterns yaw
in sapphire
dusk. The moon a glistening scar.

Photosynthesis

*for Kate Light, 1960–2016. She was a librettist, lyricist, and
poet. She was also a professional violinist & a member of the
orchestra of the New York City Opera.*

Knowing that want
      is rarely sated, we whittle

our bodies into violins, our vibrations
      into concerti.

Photon angels caress failing flesh
      with green bows.

In some languages, *leaf* and *page*
      are the same. Imagine poems

& lyrics inscribed on leaves' nervure.
      Imagine plowing earth

from left to right, a script writing
      silences between words.

Light's notation strums branches
      like violin strings. Elegies

embody spring's return, scrawl
      with chartreuse flames.

Angels emboss human veins.

The Eidolon

The psyche, she insists, swarms
in the world of things.
There are children from islands, she claims,
who are islands.
There are youths from pastoral towns
who *are* those towns.
There are elders of a forest
who *are* that brittle forest.
There are people who cry
arpeggios.
The flute is the instrument
of a freshet, its watery chant.
Are there cellos in October trees,
branches strung like strings?
Are there oboes in twilight silhouette?
The claret robe of the woman
seated in her chamber
is an invisible eidolon of that chamber,
seen.

Winter's Photogravure

Sheer birth into sheer sight:
        Voluptuous death blooms.
        Ghost membrane.

X-rayed thoughts: the unseen
        perceived. All sculpture
        has an armature, all flesh

a spine. Like delicate bones,
        a winter forest etched
        on the gelatin plates

of photogravure.
        Light feeding.
        Light consumed.

A Balm in Gilead?

for Bayard Rustin

On a street where it's always
summer, on a day
when it's always 1948,
your song rises into ether:
"There Is a Balm in Gilead."

Even though I never
knew you, your singing
calls me. My ears consume
the timbre of your spirituals.
When your words

soared to India, you met
Mahatma Gandhi, his ache
glowing from him like sacred
ash. Your pores drank
the anointing. Back

in Jim Crow America, you beamed
beatific. You fell into the caress,
the undress of a darkened car.
Headlines shrieked, "Perversion,"
as if to scour you away

with the bristles of that word.
Despite breeding, despite
patrician features, &

that sacred meeting, you
were deemed "pariah." Even

as you organized civil
rights marches (changing
the DNA of our soil),
you were erased.
As TV flickered from black-

&-white to color, you embraced
your white, male lover,
your hair gray as a chalky
blackboard. Your chant
swelled above narrative,

no longer your own. Your hymns shone
as you survived disgrace:
expulsion from history
because of whom you loved.
Now, your disembodied

song summons me: I can't
refrain from righting
you onto paper where you
illumine us with the perfect
audacity of your voice.

Daughter of Heaven & Hearth

1917: Fabergé eggs shattered. Dead butterflies
flew out, darkened the sky, petaled
eyes of imperial statues.

The French glaze that had permeated the Russian world,
eroded, scoured all that came before. A pair of revolutions
dismantled Tsarist autocracy,

led to the rise of the Soviet Union. Born in 1900,
Nabokov entered young adulthood when revolutions
ripped Tsars into bronze shards.

Crushed jewels dusted pores. Red
posters propelled propaganda. Mechanical grimaces
ground poems. *Deus ex machina:* a new idol—Stalin.

Gallic pages crumbled & blew away as the Soviet Union
bled. Nabokov first called forth *Speak, Mnemosyne:*
Goddess of memory, mother of Zeus,

daughter of Heaven & Earth.
The memoir sprouted into *Speak, Memory,*
written in English, translated into Russian's

glistering words. Ash
fell like black snow.
Bodies burning.

The Missing

after Untitled, *a photograph by Jerry N. Uelsmann*

To sphere is boundary,
a pointed darkness,
host of declarations.

One would be wrong to call the globe
"sun," or, simply because it's round,
"moon." It waits

among rags of cloud—grayed chaos.
The bottom of the orb is congealed.
The eye reads it as a dark river.

At the shore, an empty skiff heaves out, in
on gelatinous waters.
What happened to the person

in the boat? Did water quaff
the doll-like body? Inside the glassy
shell, staticked substance churns:

A face in a crystal ball?
A head appears to sit
atop shoulders & arms

as if the essence
of the missing person haunts
the fractured waves.

Shell

A brief stutter of wings
is all we recall
of a locust's life.
A crisp hull

is all we recall—
molded in the form of its inhabiter.
A crisp hull remains:
construct to retain.

Molded in the form of inhibitors,
memories crust, separate.
The construct to retain love
is the cradle of our hands.

Memories crust & separate
from our present, yet we won't let go.
Does cradling fragments in our hands
reclaim what might've been?

The present (*let go!*)
encases our locust lives,
to reclaim what might have been
during our flutter of wings.

October

In October, living sighed.
Cats slunk
& the soul brushed against buttonwood bark
as thought brushes against the mind
that it is moored to.
Branches writhe like Martha Graham

or Thai dancers, balancing
golden headdresses, rain measured by darkening
sky. Pawprints lead in circles
under sky, rust cresting.
Finally, a face appears by a broken window.

It has come to remind me of the shedding
of selves. Colors flared, flare.
The personae we were
& are dance a *pavane*
of repeating circles,
rotating like the earth.

Errant Fervor

Day subsides
with the swoosh
of a glinting angel.
I cry out—
my presence faceted.

A sullen wish
emerges (shrill!).
As I parade my empty suit,
it runs past me,
the years vacant.

There's no way to fail, flail
this lightless refraction
till water leaps.
I awaken—words
welded by flame.

Summer morning
tall with fireflies.
I gaze
at a glazed Vermeer,
: ago.

The painter of portraits
abandons daubs,
broken color, coloratura.
Shall I wait
for generous arms?

113

Dean Kostos

This year (& millennia before)
Fibonacci syllables
decipher
Sanskrit prosody—
its florid scansion.

While I'm here,
you're
immured in memory.
How feathery light
becomes.

A peacock shrieks
in opalescent dew, traipses
past a monastery perched
on a cliff—hungry winds—
island midair: Meteora.

Errant fervor—
too rusty to scrape—too
sorrowed. No one can spirit
skies & leaves.
Iridescence.

Now I sing pewter rain.
I wake the world's brutal beauty.
We disguise each other's haloes.
Winged beast,
balletic palsy.

Rooftops hide angels'
neon geometry.
Balconies support
the gawk of tourists.
For want of touch,

lips press lips.
The moon sweeps
along waves,
Atlantic gale: dark
crenellations.

Dean Kostos

Entreaty

for Ray Gast

May the winds
carving today protect you
from the noise of calendars.

May dancers flounce
their quadrilles.
May you breathe

the moon's pewter,
knowing nights recur,
dipped in dusk.

May you speak:
Shall & shall not.
May you number breaths

as forgetfulness subtracts
them &, like the infant
prophet in his coracle,

may you float from psyche
to cycle, to the shoreline
of your being.

Notes

Broken color: This brush technique was incorporated into the Impressionists' paintings during the 19th century. The color was painted on a canvas using small, short strokes (versus the normal method of carefully blending the tones and colors together). The strokes gave the visual effect of light falling over objects and figures, blending optically rather than literally.

"Charon's Response": *Hare* is the vocative form of Haros. In Modern Greek, he represents the Angel of Death. In Ancient Greek, he is Charon the ferryman who conveyed the souls of the dead across the Styx. The refrain, *Hare Mou, Pare Me* (pronounced, *Haray mou, paray may*) signifies, "Haros, take me."

Yiaya: Greek for "grandmother."

The *sávano* gown is worn by pilgrims baptized in the Jordan River. It is then used for burial. My grandmother made her *sávano*.

"Archaic Smile": Acts 17:22–31. *Then Paul stood in the midst of Mars' Hill, and said, "You men of Athens, I perceive that in all things you are too superstitious. For as I passed by, and beheld your devotions, I found an altar with this inscription: TO THE UNKNOWN GOD.*

"Yannis Ritsos": Churches under the jurisdiction of Archbishop Damaskinos were ordered by him to distribute Christian baptismal certificates to Jews fleeing the Nazis, thus saving thousands of Jews in and around Athens.

Eadweard Muybridge, April 9th, 1830, to May 8th, 1904, was an English photographer important for his pioneering work in photographic studies of motion, and early work in motion-picture projection. He influenced painters such as Marcel Duchamp.

Muybridge is known for his work on animal locomotion, which used multiple cameras to capture motion in stop-motion photographs, In the 1880s, he entered a productive period at the University of Pennsylvania in Philadelphia, producing over 100,000 images of animals and humans in motion, capturing what the human eye could not distinguish as separate movements.

"Pictures of the Floating World"

Noh: classic Japanese dance-drama having a heroic theme, a chorus, and highly stylized action, costuming, and scenery.

Ukiyo-e, literally "Pictures of the Floating World," is a genre of Japanese art which flourished from the 17th through 19th centuries. Its artists produced woodblock prints and paintings of such subjects as women, kabuki actors and sumo wrestlers.

White camellia (*tsubaki*): a flower that signifies waiting.

"The Ear Speaks, the Mouth Listens"—Paul Valéry

Acknowledgments

Acoustic Levitation: "The Doll God" and "Us-Ward"

America: The Jesuit Review of Faith and Culture: "Undoer of Knots"

The American Journal of Poetry: "El Greco" "Francis Bacon" "Frida Kahlo" "Paula Rego" "J.M.W. Turner" and "Jacopo Tintoretto"

BigCityLit: "Awabi Fishers" and "The Hobby Horse"

First Literary Review-East: "Entreaty" and "Winter's Photogravure"

From Pushkin to Pussy Riot—Russian Political Poetry & Prose: "Daughter of Heaven & Earth"

Good Men Project: "A Balm in Gilead?"

Impossible Archetype: "Motion Observed: Eadweard Muybridge"

Levure Littéraire: "Charon's Response," "Medicinal Corridors," "Soir Bleu: Six Perspectives" and "Yannis Ritsos" (originally published with a different title)

Matter: "Daughter of Heaven & Earth"

Presence: "The Coat That Wore a Man"

Sensitive Skin: "David Byrne"

Shrew: "At Janus's Gate"

With great pleasure, I thank James Bassi, Michael McKeon Bondhus, Davidson Garrett, Ray Gast, David Groff, Penelope Karageorge, Ron Kolm, Danny Lawless, Mary Ann Buddenberg Miller, Sharon Olinka, Molly Peacock, Nicholas Samaras, Larissa Shmailo, Tod Thilleman, Marc Vincenz, Don Yorty, and Michael T. Young.

Biographical Data

Dean Kostos's memoir—*The Boy Who Listened to Paintings*—was recently released; it was his ninth book, a finalist in the Foreword Indies Award. His most recent poetry collection is *Pierced by Night-Colored Threads*. His previous books include *This Is Not a Skyscraper* (recipient of the Benjamin Saltman Poetry Award, selected by Mark Doty), *Rivering, Last Supper of the Senses, The Sentence That Ends with a Comma*, and the chapbook *Celestial Rust*. He coedited *Mama's Boy* (a Lambda Book Award finalist) and edited *Pomegranate Seeds* (its debut reading was held at the United Nations). He was the recipient of a Rockefeller Foundation Cultural Innovation grant.

His poems and personal essays have appeared in over 300 journals and anthologies, such as *Boulevard, Chelsea, Cimarron Review, The Dos Passos Review, Mediterranean Poetry* (Sweden), *New Madrid, Memoir Journal, Southwest Review, Stand Magazine* (UK), *Storyscape Journal, Western Humanities Review*, and on Oprah Winfrey's website Oxygen.com. His choral text, *Dialogue: Angel of War, Angel of Peace*, was set to music by James Bassi and performed by Voices of Ascension. His literary criticism has appeared on the Harvard University Press website and elsewhere. A multiple Pushcart-Prize nominee, he served as literary judge for Columbia University's Gold Crown Awards and received a Yaddo fellowship. He is the recipient of a Rockefeller Cultural Innovation grant.

He has taught at Wesleyan, The Gallatin School of NYU, and The City University of New York. His poem "Subway Silk" was translated into a film by Jill Clark and screened at Tribeca and at the San Francisco Indiefest. He presented his paper "Schemes and Schemata: Endless Play" and read his poems at Harvard's Mahindra Humanities Center. He has also read his poetry at Princeton and City Lights Bookstore.